LOVE PARASITE

GANESH BABU CHITTILLA

This Write is Dedicated to Kanmani, I havent spent a moment without thinking about you, Your happiness is what I adore for, You couldnt be the ink of my pen but you have driven me to write back again. You truely deserve this.

Contents

1. Bride's Boyfriend ... 1

2. Love Note ... 4

3. Love Happening ... 7

4. Much Awaited Arrival ... 12

5. Is Love Alive? ... 16

6. 4:40 ... 18

7. In Search Of Lost Heart ... 21

8. Frozen Heart ... 25

9. Revive? ... 33

10. Unspoken Love ... 37

11. Wedding Bells ... 40

Epilogue ... 43

ONE
BRIDE'S BOYFRIEND

Visakhapanam,

It's a dark and cloudless sky dotted with white spots twinkling at me. Full moon gleaming and stars shining and lending their luminosity to the late evening sky. The dark blue water bathes in the ivory of the moon, the huge square shaped rocks on which I'm sitting were at the harbour of Visakhapatnam, beach road and late night city lights adds more beauty to the view. Heavy breeze and the waves striking the rocks with brute force right in front of me. Every cigarette I lit was burning quicker than usual, I've already gulped in a couple of beers which gives enough booze to my brain. Something is spinning in my brain and It was her wedding today, I remember Raghav telling me that Aarthi is going to get married and that's why I was here in Visakhapatnam, I've checked my mobile and there were 7 missed calls, I'm in no mood to check who all called me, I knew that it was my friends waiting for me to attend the wedding. How could I attend and wish my ex-girlfriend a good life with someone else. I made my way back to my

Royal Enfield kick start it, I'd rather choose to power start but I wanted to release my aggression a bit, released the clutch and drove to the Convention named WED-DESTINATION. Where have you been yelled Raghav spotting me and I don't want any conversation with him now. Saurabh hey you bastard yelled another and there were another 4 of our childhood friends and then I've made my way inside. God she's Stunning, I couldn't take my eyes off her. It's my childhood wish to see her in traditional Hindu Bridal getup and my eyes captured those visuals and thoughts hovering in my brain, how on earth was the idiot standing beside her is better than me, I shrugged that only Indian fathers have the superpowers to find a dumb-ass as their son-in-law. My thoughts broke apart when I feel a touch on my shoulder and a voice from behind, Saurabh how are you, asked Mahita, my childhood best friend, she got married a couple of years ago and left to Germany with her husband. Hey Mahi, how are you doing I asked with a heavy heart and wet eyes. She was more concerned how I'd react to Aarthi's wedding and not just her everyone in my peer group. Aarthi and I met for the first time at the Pollocks Higher Secondary School. She looked so adorable in blue and white coloured uniform, a girl who just turned into an adolescent. Her sparkling eyes with blemishing cheeks and baby pink lips and her smile, probably best in the world made me fall for her at the first moment. I was a troublesome and notorious kid and my teachers always had a pile of complaints on me and they transfer them as virus into my parents' brains and their computers will obviously treat me with an antivirus called leather belt, How sweet. I was beaten up by my father for forgery of his signature on my report card and my father lost his cool, gifted me a couple of hard hitting leather striking my young and white skin which turned dark blue and the pain was excruciating. I wanted to go out for some time to see my friends and it was then I spoke to Aarthi for the first time, she was dressed up in light green and white chudidhar, perfectly matched to her skin tone and her loose hair made her look so captivating. Raghav and I were discussing about the sports meet which was about to take place the next week, being the Head Boy Raghav has some duties assigned by the teachers and then comes Aarthi asking about the participation formalities, I interrupted Raghav and took over the responsibility of explaining to this most beautiful girl, later that we had casual conversation with her smiling all the time and I kept staring at her, she was the most beautiful girl I've ever known. Aarthi and I used to meet at the park every evening, that was the most awaited time of the day, not even the sports period made me so excited than seeing her at the park, having Ice cream with her and spending time with the girl I love the most, I couldn't convey my love to her as our budding bonding may end.

TWO
LOVE NOTE

New Delhi,

I was at my balcony where the sun melting down the hills adding its luminescence to the sky which turned into pale pint of Orange, I moved to Delhi along with my family 4 years ago. Aarthi promised she will keep in touch on social media and I haven't proposed to her yet...! I left her when a half formed tear drop hanging down her sparkling eyes, where I packed the other half of my heart under my polo tee. It has been ages since we've met I remember the warmth on her palms, the fragrance of her hair, her outspoken eyes and her fragile lips with a sly smile on them. My mom became a close companion whereas my Businessman dad has got no time for me. He is a person with a different mind-set which sets him apart from other fathers. His unconditional love towards me and the ample of time which he speaks with me about life is enough to create a different approach on how I live my life. I enrolled in Delhi University for my Undergrad degree in Architecture and Architectonics. Aarthi went to University of British Colombia for her studies. We were some thousands of miles apart where I feel our hearts are connected through an invisible thread which binds us together. I was at the Library going through the thesis when my friend Akhil whispered did you see her, Shreya the most beautiful young lady in the University campus, god might have taken a lot of effort to shape her into perfection, ah.. why so much fuss about a girl bro she was a creature too I said without even looking her. You never know her, you'll definitely get carried away by her looks Akhil said with a hysterical face. She's coming this way he said with a higher tone adjusting his hair and it was that moment I looked at her a girl in pinkish white skin tone, brown hair covered half of her face, deep eyes with thick eyelashes layered by oval shaped glasses, pink lips smile making her cheeks to blemish, that girl in blue dress who turned things very nervous for me. "Okay, man she's cute what's her name by the way" I asked Akhil, "Shreya" he said, where a sarcastic smile lingered on his face. Its a weekend eve after the class I was waiting for Sundar, my friend who's gonna join for outing. I was in my car at the University parking lot my earphones playing loud western music and my eyes scanning the thesis papers. My eyes shifted attention all of a sudden towards Shreya, I just noticed her face but, I started to wonder how could a one decide to live the whole freaking life with another, how do they have strength, confidence and trust on their partner does the word "love" mean that much, handing your complete time, happiness, grief, joy almost half of your life to spend with them. In this world of 7.9 billion people spreading over 197 countries how does one know that their partner is the one, a whole lot of confusion I shrugged. Sundar and I drove to Bahi pub, there's something mocking in my mind in constant but nothing is clear about it come on man take a deep breath I said to myself and asked for a beer at the bartender. Look at her eyes son, not everyone has the spark only the one who's born for you will have it and you'll meet her and that's destiny my dad said on a late weekend eve. Love was never so sweet in my life so far I wanted a girl who was pole apart and checking out on an another so called college beauty, why am I so confused about girls I asked myself. Shreya came looking for me after the class as she found my book in the college canteen which has my thoughts and how much I'd love my girl, it's a kind of a very personal note, I never know that I misplaced it. Shreya said cute while handling my book back with a prettiest smile, Did you read it I asked with a pint of excitement lingering on she said that girl would be so lucky and waved off where my eyes kept staring at her until she disappeared from the horizon. Smile on my face remembering Aarthi, everything in this note is for her but never outspoken. The book had a sticky note which has shreya's number and a smiley face scribed on. I didn't make an effort to save it as my heart was desperate for Aarthi. I knew that I was madly in love with her and expressing it was not my cup of tea.

THREE
LOVE
HAPPENING

New Delhi,

I was in the final semester of my graduation and my college is about to end, the feeling of missing this college and more importantly friends started in my heart, while sipping my coffee in the college cafeteria. I noticed Shreya coming my way and she took the opposite seat of my table wishing me, I too wished her she asked didn't you see my number in your notes, I've noticed it but I dragged on why didn't you text me I was expecting your message that day itself she said Yup I wasn't so close to you and I wanted to text you after getting to know you a bit I said. She took her mobile out from her bag and checked it and I minded my business until a notification beeped from my mobile. Now you can text me back she said and I had a smile on my face and replied Hello, we texted as the magical conversation box muted the world around it even unvoiced us too, words rolled on WhatsApp chat rather than uttering out sitting right in front of her and talking to her on chats was so funny at the end of the day, same cafeteria, table and chairs and the same means of conversation had became routine to us. I was never so outspoken with Shreya even though I started to feel every step she takes leading to my heart which was reserved for Aarthi. With all the silly confusions in my mind I don't want to screw my friendship with her, moreover I wasn't so sure about relationship yet. We used to hang out more and roamed around the city and then the calendar ticked the time of our exams, I don't study hours won't last for hours just some highlighted topics and graphs. The final semester in the college dissolved in quick time where I was awaiting to start my professional career, the campus drive was round in the corner and I was really excited and nervous to land in my dream job. The Morphosis, my dream Architecture firm, A US based MNC was also a part of this campus drive to recruit young talent. I was thriving to be a part of them and prepared really well for their interview procedures and did my own research and got to know about their establishments and achievements. The D day has come I was sitting to be called in for the interview and the nervousness is sky rocketing, my heart beat is at a rapid pace, the sweat rolling down my forehead and neck and my brain is trembling, I noticed a shiver in my knees and god this is stress I murmured and took a long breath. My body shook when my name was called in and I went in and shut the door behind me, I came back out after 30 or 40 minutes and I was confident enough that I made it. After a week or so I received a call from the recruitment team and said I got selected and the offer letter would be rolled out soon. There were no limits to my happiness and I felt like I was on top of the world. My parents celebrated on me achieving my dream job. My college appreciated all the selects from the drive and yeah there were many greetings received, the one from Shreya was a bit more special as she called me her superstar in the party which I threw at a pub. I was at the lounge had to take a call and Shreya followed me out of the dance floor and I didn't notice her, she was waiting behind me to finish the call and came to me after, I said hey you enjoyed? How do you think I would enjoy without you she replied with her eyes locked straight into mine, establishing a deep eye contact she came close to me and said congratulations darling, I said thank you and she hugged me. I too hugged her back and we went back in we danced a lot, boozed enough. I drove her back home. That night while I was driving back the revving sounds of my Triumph street triple where I feel the fresh breeze on my face and speeding made my eyes watery, I was thinking more about love these days I never let my heart out with Aarthi whereas I feel getting attracted to Shreya, this confusing mind is enough to let your heart make a wrong move, I was clear in what I wanted. The final exams are in the corner and I finished my thesis all set to take the final exams. One evening I was in my room sketching the modern commercial spaces plans my phone beeped with a ton of unread messages, but one grabbed my attention as it was from Aarthi. I kept on texting her for an hour and Shreya kept on calling me constantly, I picked her call and she shouted congratulations sweetheart besides the wish I really enjoyed her excitement. Why so I asked, you bagged the highest package in your whole batch havent you checked your offer she asked, I will call you back I said and ran through my inbox where my offer was on top of the mailbox. There were absolutely no words after watching the figures listed, I felt like achieving something great. Final exams were done and I performed really well. Thoughts were really clear now and I went to my graduation with my head held high were I could see happy smiles around me. Leaving the University I turned back where I could see younger me standing at the gate for the first day of my college with tonnes of confusions where a better me leaving the campus, that's what colleges teach us apart from education, I felt lost in the millions of memories that I had in my bag to embrace in the rest of my life. I had a two month gap to my date of joining so I wanted to visit my grandparents back in Visakhapatnam. Shreya called for a meetup before I leave, I picked her up and drove to Digin Cafe. She looked pretty cute in her cute white t-shirt paired with a pale blue jeans and a very classy looking casual sandals. Her eyes kept staring into mine than usual she wasn't so talkative today which was pretty irregular a chatterbox keeping silent doesn't match the regular vibe. Hey you're more into girls who dress up traditionally right? she asked what why is she so different today I shrugged. Is she the special one am I not able to figure it out, is this love same sort of questions hovering in my cobwebbed brain while I was sipping my hot chocolate. I know I'm not ready for any kind of relationship with this sort of questions in my brain but what if I loose her, I cant afford let her leave out of my life. I don't want a conversation about relationship and girls now I'm confused Shreya I said, and she talked various things, we kept on smiling through out, One thing is clear this girl will bring the smile to the corner of my lips at the end of the day, she is the sort of the girl that every guy deserves. Who doesn't want a peaceful time after being stressed out at work I thought and we left. My gaze towards her changed since then her eyes damn I always wanted to look at them, I waved a bye hugging her. Enough of confusion its high time to decide, Lemme confess to Aarthi first let's see how it goes anyways Shreya know that

I've got my eyes on Aarthi. I boarded the flight to Visakhapatnam with a heavy baggage in my brain, I'm very desperate to know what the hell LOVE IS? Do you have an answer....

FOUR

MUCH AWAITED ARRIVAL

Visakhapatnam,

Cool breeze kissing my forehead, caressing my wavy hair, waves whirling with a beautiful gush sweeping off the sand beneath my wet toes, starboard lights of ships over the horizon, I could hear my heart beat generating pace as I wanted to let my heart out to Aarthi, but I wish to make it in person. I will make my heart wait until she comes back to India. I was here in Visakhapatnam to see my grandparents as it's been so long I've visited them. I had enough time to think and make decisions on my love life, I always know that Aarthi was meant for me but confusions always pop up in youngsters mind. My grandmother was so excited to see me in here and showered lots of love which I've missed so much. I love and adore the chemistry between my grandparents they were the best couple I ever know. I wish to see an ocean of love like them. One night at the dinner table I asked my grandfather how could he love granny so much and how was the chemistry possible between you two, my granny laughed aloud and threw a glance at me and said, son if you wish to see an ocean of love you should have the courage to swim across in it, you'll not know the depth of it until you jump into it and you'll get the courage if you have faith and trust on your partner and that deep relation you have with her is called love. I was baffled with an answer like this and unknown what to say next, Maybe this is an answer to my everlasting question. My grandfather asked don't you have a girlfriend till now? You should have dated many by now he said laughing. Yes I would have dated many if I want but I want love grandpa not every girl these days offers it I said with a smile sparkling on my face. He had a sly smile on his face while he finished his roti. What are you still single, Delhi girls were model material bro fast too, If I were you I would have many girlfriends bro said Raghav. I laughed out loud and said I don't want a temporary girlfriend dude I had lots of expectations on her I want someone special, ah come on bro just for dates you should have gone you're missing a lot of fun you can't do it later, this is the age to enjoy said Raghav with a weird expression. Puberty hits hard to everyone it happened to me as well but I never wanted someone on my bed it should happen with great romance and chemistry, I never adapted that chemistry with anyone and I wanted Aarthi to be my wife you know that and still speaking shit I said staring straight into his expressionless face. Do you still love her asked Raghav and I said Yes without second thought, I will express whenever she comes back. Don't you know she's coming this week said Raghav. My excitement was skyrocketing and my face turned bright like sun. I don't want her to know that I was in Visakhapatnam. I kept on chatting with her without letting her know about my whereabouts she was so excited for her visit back home, we kept on texting for so long reliving our childhood days together, this time with her was the best as the distance between us is reducing at rapid pace even though we were 7 seas apart. I waited so long for the day of her arrival, I kept on texting late night until she boarded the flight. A part of my heart is coming back to me in the next 16 hours I shrugged before my eyes shut. It wasn't a comfortable sleep where my overexcited brain kept on thinking about Aarthi's arrival. This sunrise is the best I've ever seen I said while sipping coffee with my grandmother, Raghav is here honking for me and I rushed kissing my granny. I took the steering of black Skoda Kodiaq and my foot kept on pressing the accelerator until we reach the airport. I know I'm not going to face her but I wish to see her, I still remember waving to her in the same airport it's been 4 long years since distance broke us apart. The announcement about the arrival of her flight made things very nervous for me. At this point of time I have two options one is to surprise her and other is to see her from distance, I asked my brain to surprise her and now the plan was different I immediately rushed to get a bouquet. Raghav and I were waiting for her at the arrival and my heart was eager, eyes searching for that one person I've thrived for and then spotted her. Things went numb around me, I could feel absolute silence around me, could feel butterflies staring my Aarthi in a black t-shirt layered in a hoodie and a pair of jeans with, her cute face clearly carrying two emotions, restless travelling and a whole lot of excitement to meet her dear ones. I made my way towards her every step I take felt like crossing each ocean which separated us, my heart beat thumping to tell her. I said hey Aarthi, welcome back home handing the bouquet. Her eyes filled with sheer surprise to see me here, she hugged me tight, our eyes locked into each-others' deep contact into her eyes threw me out of this world, I wanted those eyes forever. Her parents were amused to see her, I cherished those moments standing behind her holding my hands, everything felt like a romantic bollywood movie. Raghav patted me and said not every story has a happy ending bro, his words shook the happy side of me and assumptions started to knock my mind, Will my story have a happy ending? Eww this author had already given this answer in the first lines itself.... Anyways that' s not the end of my story.

FIVE

IS LOVE ALIVE?

Visakhapatnam,

The Late night sky cloud casted with half moon shining so far away, thoughts of Arathi hovering around me and my heart carrying her weight. Slowly injecting into my veins and pumping into my heart, then my mind says yes SHE IS THE ONE. The long wait is over and the day I wanted to let my feelings to her. She asked for a meet up after a long week of meeting relatives and friends and then came my turn. Well did I tell you about her, a cute little and friendly heart who spreads love around her, I've never seen a woman like her. That night while playing a game Raghav asked her to tell a few lines about me. All eyes are curious about her answer she gaze towards me and I stood still awaiting for a reply then rolled out words from her mouth stating that " Ram... who has the wavy dark hair... which flutters with the cool breeze of this night.. his black eyes which has many words hidden, behind the darkness.. driving me to somewhere special, And I wish those words behind the darkness should be for me... I will wait for that moment. The time when his silence break into words.. " Those words made me feel so special to her everyone around are amused for her words which made her intentions very clear. Raghav shouted like hell and congratulated me. I couldn't respond to him as I was very busy collecting bits of our unspoken love, looking into her eyes I understood it's a YES without a proposal, the formality of uttering my feelings is still pending. Then and there itself I walked to her Will you come on a drive with me, I asked. A very little nod and a cute smile said yes. Empty highway while a little drizzle making the atmosphere cool while the moon light shed its beauty to the route ahead where I was wheezing through the road where the exhaust of my street triple making a beautiful melody. The stage is perfect to express those lines said my heart. I've carried the ring which I brought for her today as I anyways wanted to let my heart out. I closed her eyes and walked her down to my place, the water view front. She was amused to see the water falls pouring down to the stream, my palms searched for the little box of ring hiding in my pocket. I have kneeled down in front of her." I never know what love really is but you were definitely the meaning of love in my life. If it's not you then its no one else Aarthi. I love you tonnes that my heart couldn't carry anymore, I started to love you since childhood but realized it late. Will you marry me" I said. She extended her palm and said yes I love you too Ram I will marry you. If not you then no one else. She hugged me tight and her warmth made the things around me magical, I wanted to see the rest of the world with her leaping into her shoulder, finally my long stretched love story had a grand beginning. That night I realized that what is truly meant for you will find its way into your life. I always wanted Aarthi to be mine and it happened. Yes my love is alive I replied to myself before hitting the bed.

SIX

4:40

Barcelona, Spain.

Busy streets, rushing public, vibrant culture and white powered faces, fresh fragrances in the air where the early spring breeze brushing the trees on either sides of the busy LA RAMBLA street, busiest street in the city of Barcelona. People rushing with their lives covered in blazers, semi coats, top branded things from head to toe, running around Euros. The faces that hardly carry any emotions, I could only see the raw emotions only in children. Sadly even after realizing all these I was one among them, Standing on a skyscraper covered on glass which resembles the mask I put on. It's been 2 years since I stepped in Spain, living the best life, luxury car, 6 figure earning, a modern self deigned home, what else do anyone wish for in life. Yes I agree this is the life everyone wish for and work hard for luckily I've earned my dream life. It's been 3 years since I found myself dead where the body is living without its soul. At the end of the day I don't find love beside me, What am I doing with my life, all this hard work, everything I did to be in this position doesn't matter when there is no one beside you, these thoughts spinned in my mind. Time heals Saurabh, said Rekha aunty patting my shoulder, The best gift that god gave to mankind is to forget things. The pain you're carrying on your heart isn't that easy to forget it takes time look how you've changed after that. Try to let her go out of your heart and mind son you should be fine soon shall we leave to the workplace she said. I nodded and we made our way to my office. Rekha aunty one of the greatest woman I came across in my life, being my project manager she was the senior at the workplace and a second mother, Deepak uncle I never missed my parents in my time here its only because of you two I said while sharing the bottle of wine with them. They stood beside me in my tough times and helped me throughout. Son Saurabh we love you so much I wanted to know what's in your heart tonight, I've never seen you smile with your heart even though in your success and growth you're lost in something, as you said were you're parents share it with us he said sipping his drink. His words threw me back in time to the very next day after Aarthi said yes. Her stay in India was around 2 months and she will head back to Canada for her final semester classes. We had a very great emotional connect in between us I don't even remember how time flew and the day she was leaving arrived even before my flight back to Delhi. I was so low when I met her for the last time felt like loosing a piece of my heart. I was at the airport searching for her. Her parents are around along with some friends and family she waved a bye from distance and I still remember that moment. Uncle my relationship lasted just for few years but she showcased the love, care and affection which made me feel 4 years like the rest of 40. I never knew that day at the airport was the last time I see her as mine and the next time I saw her is at her wedding. It was an emotional roller coaster where I was trying to hide my pain where my heart is struggling to beat in its rhythm and I was trying to act normal. Too heavy to handle said Uncle Deepak keeping away his glass came to me and hugged me. The pain which you took in your past will always make you a better in life, look where you are now how you are doing but I think you are still carrying something in your heart son, if you let that out you'll be fine. Go on a trip son find yourself who's lost in the past, question him what he really wants and time will teach you what you really are and what purpose you really serve. Come back to me with a bag of memories and the pure smile I'll wait for you until then, come on lets have dinner now said uncle Deepak. That night while driving back home uncle's words kept me busy until my driver said were home sir. I was at the office the next day after finishing my meeting Rekha aunt came to me and said what are your thoughts on going for a trip as Deepak said last night? I'm on it aunty don't know where to go I wanted to go to Canada I said. I could see something in her eyes she didn't said anything to me but I know she doesn't want me to go to the place where Aarthi is. I was at the airport waiting for my flight at the lounge, I saw a young girl she must be over 3 years she was playing with some dolls, her cute smile her every action made my eyes struck onto her. Her tiny little feet kept on running around and at that moment I realized I stopped running with my life long back. I was standing still at a moment where the life around me was moving and I lagged back. I had a very great time with that little girl named Aaradhya, she was the sole responsible for teaching me to laugh back again with my heart. I was in my flight, forty thousand feet above the ground thinking Aarthi would have a child who would be in the same age of Aaradhya. A thought blossomed in my mind which I never had before, What if I meet Aarthi again?

SEVEN

IN SEARCH OF
LOST HEART

Vancuover,

Early morning sun just rose in the coldest whether where the freezing temperatures making me shiver where I took in a deep breath and smog came out of my nose, City covered in thick layer on snow. I reached my hotel The Westinn Bayshore in an hour its was faced on the cruise terminal side of the bay. I took a walk around the bay, frozen crystals resembled my broken heart. My headphones playing Telugu music from my old classic playlist I placed myself on a wooden bench and lost myself in the music for a while and Strolled around the busy streets of the city. It's been a week since my arrival I have visited every tourist spots in the city I walked around Stanley park, skied down the snow covered Grouse Mountain, took a ride on Aquabus, roamed around the glass planed skyscrapers and I'm fed up living in cities, I wanted to visit the countryside. Most of the Canadians live in the cities, enough of modern loneliness, there will be a huge area to explore in the countryside. I found myself in a bus to Merrickvillie, Ontario. It feels like the whole country is painted in white, the dense layer of snow covered the whole place. I checked into a motel, just a casual one. Feels great staying far from luxury. Placed myself near the fireside in my room, I asked myself all the answers for the unanswered questions. Living my life in an unknown place where I have become a stranger to myself, finding myself alone even there were people around. An hour passed my brain have no answers but the memories of Aarthi in it, she kept on flashing in front of my eyes. Time will heal you they say but it kept on hurting me the most, I could do nothing for time to answer all my questions. My brain threw myself back to the past after Aarthi left to Canada, The smile on my face departed along with her. The next day I have received a text from her saying that she have reached her dorm and tired, there were a quick two minute texts and later on she fell asleep. I missed her so badly that i have been to every place where we were together carrying a missing piece of my heart, nothing felt like before and the communication gap between us has many factors like her classes, different time zones and her being too tired. I have boarded my flight back to Delhi waving back to my grandparents. I still remember my grandpa saying "Ram, Love always finds its way into your life don't ever search for it when the time comes it knocks your heart, you'll know if its love and you don't need to express it in your words. If she is the one she will get to know that" Focus on your career do well son" he said Hugging me. I put on a very happy face then and said your words are true grandpa. I have landed back in Delhi, I don't even have a thought of Shreya during my time in Vizag but now She was at the airport to pick me up. I was surprised to see her waiting for me with a ply card holding welcome back my hero, that moment I realized that I have probably landed myself in trouble. Confusion started in my brain, Shreya came running to me and hugged me and I was standing still with no clue about what is going to happen. I was in a dilemma whether to tell Shreya about my relationship with Aarthi, how would Shreya take it. What if Shreya is into me, will it end up in a bad way? Huh not now will tell her whenever time comes I have decided to take time on this topic. Shreya I have to talk something important I have texted her on a late evening the day before joining into my job. Shall we meet she said immediately, I asked her to come to the Rajpath park near the India Gate while powering on my street triple. Green fields, pathway leading to the beautiful India Gate densely covered with thick layer of fog, street lamps shedding light into the fog where cool breeze is skimming past our bodies. Shreya I have to talk I said and she was expecting to hear love, I was trying so hard to confess her about my relationship with Aarthi. Shreya kept on speaking something about her goals, aspirations, music, her college stories and all, I tried to break my silence and You know Aarthi na I said, yeah how do you think I don't know about her I'll tell about her in 3 lines, Your school days crush, you got to path ways in middle as you've shifted to Delhi and She was in Canada now, Right she said hopping on to a bench. Yes She came to India recently and we have spent time together and I.. We... I took a pause for a while, She said yes I said. I was looking straight into her eyes, there was an expression on her face where I couldn't understand she said congratulations yaar, I'm happy for you. I could understand that she was about break out into tears but she managed to control her emotions and she left. I was stranded unknowing of the situation, I accompanied her to her car and said I'm sorry Shreya I hope you understand what I meant. She nodded and said bye waving her hand. At that moment I had a very guilt feeling that she was so into me where I was so helpless. I could see no texts or calls for her for a week and I had a very bad feeling about that. I have called her, surprised to see I was no response from her even on social media, What on earth is happening. I have gone to the University to see her, I have asked some juniors to call her to canteen. I was waiting in the canteen having a sandwich with a cigarette in between my fingers, She came to me and said, Ram what brought you here. Why aren't you so unresponsive to me what have I done? Is everything okay? I asked. I'm okay yaar bit busy and I thought of staying away from you, I'm afraid of falling for you that is not good for both of us I think I'm done getting late to the class she said and left. I was speechless unknown what to say, my eyes keep on staring at her until she disappeared from my sight. I started to develop a feeling that Did I really gave hope to get Shreya to fall for me, Is the relation I share with Shreya is love. Umm I have joined my job and excited to see how my life unfolds.

EIGHT

FROZEN HEART

Merrickvillie,

The smoke of the burned woods around the chimney, freezing cold breeze finds its way into the dorm from an open window, Sun hiding behind the thick cloud cover, the beeping phone woke me up I noticed a call from Rekha Aunty. She started with son how are you and spoke for a while about my whereabouts and what I was feeling, the very next moment a guilt feeling started to crush me down to find what my heart wants. I feel like I'm normal from inside but people around me could clearly sense that I was not fine. Am I not able to see myself, is that the reflection in the mirror isn't mine, is something missing in my life, I wanted to exert the pain within. I walked out of the dorm and started to walk, The late monsoon winds blew past my wrinkled face and I kept walking on the lonely road by the end of the street, a Man greeted good morning gentleman, He was in his 60s dressed in black sweater, a scarf hanging down his neck and his oval glasses with a black hat on his grey haired head a perfect cut out of a very decent man. Good morning gentleman, I said with a weird expression and unknowing what to say next. He said would you mind accompanying me? I was just a tourist I'm unaware of anything here, But I don't mind joining you I too wanted to explore this place. That man greeted me nice to meet you Gentleman I'm Dr. Karl Fracnik and I shook his hand saying my name is Ram. We started to walk along that road. Where are we heading to I asked him He said I was thinking to have a coffee now there is a coffee shop right around this corner, Frappe there, would make your taste buds go high he said and a coffee lover like me would never miss out his offer. We sat at the small coffee bar and he ordered frappe for both of us, He offered me smoke and lit it for me, just after the first breath he said young man you are carrying a lot of pain inside you I could see it in your eyes, I was in a gruesome feeling right away. I pity for myself being In such a state. Yes I'm not fine Mr. Karl I was in pain but I don't know the reason for it and don't know how to overcome it. I was in search of answers but haven't found anything yet, at this point of time all I could say is I've lost myself and trying to help myself in search of me. He had a straight glared straight and he told your eyes says what you are feeling Ram. He sipping his Frappe said You know what I was here to help you, the best psychiatrist in the country is with you. I was amused I went into a feeling where Am I in need of a psychiatrist? Did something is seriously wrong with me, all these questions arose in my mind and then said Mr, Karl that don't get me wrong young man I've been observing you from past two days, we travelled on the same bus and we checked into the same motel, I could see bitterness in your eyes, I even thought of visiting you twice but I couldn't, Today I don't wanted to leave you alone, so I asked you out on for a coffee so that I could see how I could help you. I feel things so comfortable around him. I don't want to leave out on a helping hand. Ram tell me your story and I will help you in search of your answers said Mr. Karl. I started to tell him everything that I have done with my life. How I fell in Love, how I built my career and how I lost the love of my life and how I ended up in here. He listened to my story very keenly he asked me lot of questions in between and he understood how I felt in every stage of my life. The way he is now was completely different after listening to my story. After a long pause he words started to roll out of his mouth. " You have a cold blooded heart, it's been so long since red blood passed through your arteries, the pain in you turned your blood black and emotionless" you carry pain but you should understand how to come out of it, if you never try you can't find answers for your questions in your life, none the less I could say you don't even have questions in your life, for what sake you are trying to search answers for? If not lived in peace no matter where you go in this world you cannot find happiness Ram. Many people think I was a great psychiatrist but no one knows what I have been through. Even a psychiatrist has their own mental problems. I have gone through a rough patch in my life and I wish to share the story of my life with you I never felt to share it with anyone so far. When I was young, in my mid 30s I had just began to gain popularity my career just started to fly high. There were times I was busy at my office for more than 18 hours a day. I ran behind money, fame, success but all of them demolished me and crushed me to the ground so hard that even I fought depression. I was in peak of my career that I don't even use to have time for my wife or son. Juliana... (a 5 second pause) my wife, she is my childhood love and we got married, she was a wonderful woman that a man could get, We were madly in love with each other and our son Jason was the symbol of our love. I never got time for them. I missed most of his childhood but love for him is constant. I was always busy working hard to provide them a luxurious and comfortable life, I know my wife missed my presence beside her most of the times but she knew me well that all my hard work is for them. I took them on a trip once where we went on to a long road trip, I was driving where my wife is sitting with Jason in her lap. I was on a phone call while driving at 80 miles. I didn't notice the intersection where a heavy truck was joining the freeway and It was too late where the distracted me looked at the truck 5 feet away from my car and I had to brake hard steered the car to the right. I had crashed into the truck, I could only remember a loud noise of collision and darkness slowly engulfed. I opened my eyes two days later in the ICU of a hospital terribly injured and my father in law beside me, my first words were July? And my uncle kept weeping said they were no more. Silence struck around me I had pain enough to shatter to break my heart into million pieces but I don't know how to react. I was left in silence where The funeral of my wife and son happened I was sitting on a wheel chair wrapped myself in tuxedo. All my memories with them have become stories right in front of my eyes. I was all alone in my home without them. My heart carrying them, I never know that a second could change my life forever. I went into depression so badly that I started to Hallucinating their presence. It took me 5 complete months to accept the reality that they were no more. I learnt to accept that, all my feelings were memories now and I could do nothing to change them and accept life as it was. Then started the next phase in me but I still live with a frozen heart, I had gone through a lot. I don't want to see a young man like you suffer with pain and lost in past. I have seen my younger self in your eyes Ram and I thought of helping you out. Accept your reality and then your search for answer, then that really matters said Mr. Karl. I was so struck that a man who lost all his life in a second had something to offer me as help. Somewhere in a corner this planet, in an unknown place, an unknown man wanted to help me out just looking into my eyes. I stood up putting on my coat, Thanks Dr. Karl I will come to you again, I promise the next time you see me you'll find a better me, Thanks for your concern I said walking away. I spent an another week in the countryside but I never saw him again. I headed back to the airport, I'm going to Delhi to see my parents it's been 3 years since I have last met them. I have checked in and waiting at the longue for my long haul flight. I have few magazines beside me and I grabbed one, flipping the pages where I was shocked to see Mr. Karl's picture in the centre page and he was being interviewed by one of the top magazine publishers in Canada. I have then got to know that he was Canada's top psychiatrist and had won many awards for his work. I have kept that magazine in my cabin luggage and could hear giggles of a child and her anklets making beautiful gush. I turned around and noticed a kid who is hardly around 3 running away from her mother and suddenly fell on the floor. I had rushed to pick her up in the mean while her mom came running, I hold the kid trying to console her and noticed Aarthi right in front of my eyes, the bright kumkum on her forehead, her eyes locked into mine with her kid crying in between us. I had an adrenaline rush with my heart pounding with emotions. With an audacity to talk to her kicking inside where we stood in silence looking into each-others' eyes, she holding her daughter in her arms and All the emotions spoke in silence. She asked how are you, breaking the silence I have no words a simple nod, and asked you. Yeah I'm good she said, Daughter? I asked and she said yes, she's cute I mean she completely resembles you I said. Ishitha is her name said Aarthi. Umm Prudhvi? I asked. I'm going to India he was busy, couldn't make it now she said. Okay I said and an awkward silence followed. I don't know what to call this emotion or feeling that I have now, you get to understand this. I couldn't resist any more time with her and, I got to go, good to see you I said and walked back where my frozen heart started to fill the blood back in red and a tear drop hanged down my eye, and my hand wept the tear drop. I never wanted to see her again but this unexpected moment of my life reminded me that my life still SUCKS. A seat beside me left empty, Signing me that it was yet to get filled asI felt like I had a strong gut feeling that my past where I was still struck in hit me in reality.I did not have any conversation with her. I boarded my flight, hands searching the magazine which I packed earlier. I was amazed that an air hostess pointing Aarthi the aisle seat right beside me, My heart kept pounding from the very next moment. She made herself comfortable along with her sleeping baby wrapped around her hands. How are you Ram she asked, A hesitant reply uttered out of my mouth I'm fine, I asked are you really fine and doing great in life? I said yes, my life is great. You doesn't appear to be fine Ram, I always wish for your happiness though I'm not with you said Aarthi. Life had offered me everything I'm happy but what hurts me the most is I'm still carrying you in my heart, I don't know how to move on. I was still struck with you that pain cant be healed so easily Aarthi I don't know how you are but I don't want to create chaos in your life as well as my chaotic heart never let me live in peace. She kept silent for a while. I remained silent unknowing what would be her reply. She said my life took a strange turn after my wedding, The struggle I took to marry you,

I waged a war for you with my parents and was lost I was helpless and couldn't win the battle, I too had the same love towards you but my husband was a great guy his love and caring made me come over. You wont believe he didn't even touch my finger for over two years of our marriage. Ram love is not about being together forever accepting and caring for them is what love is, in that aspect my husband was a man to have. I have no words for that. Ram I know your life would be shattered after I left, but you're a star you are meant to shine munchkin (the phrase she used to call me during our relationship) I never expected that I will see you again and even at the time of my wedding I controlled myself not to cry. This meeting had enabled us to speak about how our lives were after all that, maybe this is good for us she said. I too never expected that I will meet you Aarthi, It was so great to see you after all these years I said. My life completely changed once she was born her first giggle made me forget all the pain in the world and she was the world to me. We were a small and a happy family now she said. We had spoken through out the flight about my career how I was doing with life and all, We have landed in Heathrow and the moment she was about to leave for her connecting flight to Delhi, she turned back hugged me and Ishitha kissed me on my cheek. Carrying me in your heart doesn't mean you should live at the moment of our separation. Carrying me in your smile, in your happiness and your prosperity munchkin, smile should be a permanent mark on my Ram's face. My happiness lies in your smile you said you are carrying me in your heart but not in your smile. Its time to get healed Ram I feel I was the reason to get hurt and now I was the one to heal as well. I love you till my last breath she said waving off, She left to the gate of her departure and I had to take an another gate for my flight back to Barcelona, Walking in different ways remains me of our relationship taking different paths. I boarded my flight with a smile on my face and now the airplane my eyes shut and I dozed off at 34000 feet above the sea level.

NINE
REVIVE?

Barcelona,

The busy city life surrounded by glass buildings and I was back in my life covered in concrete jungle with the memories I had packed from the snow covered mountains and green fields in Canada. My boy is back said aunt Rekha opening the door of my cabin, I missed you aunt I said Hugging her. Come home for dinner tonight my niece from India was here to see us, Ill introduce you to her said aunt before she left my cabin. I walked out to grab a burger from Bailes Brunch, Bailen Street. I was waiting to cross the road and noticed a familiar face walking on the opposite side of the road she seemed like Shreya from distance and I didn't bother that much I am pretty sure that is her but I don't want to go have a conversation with her. I left my office late was busy with lot of pending works where Rekha aunt was constantly asking me to come for dinner. I rang the door bell at Rekha aunts house. The door cracked open and a young lady opened the door looked straight into my eyes and I noticed the amusement in her eyes as she noticed me, I was shell shocked to see Shreya at Rekhas place. Here comes my darling said Rekha aunt standing at the hallway.

I was speechless at that moment. Uncle Deepak hugged me and said you seemed a lot better now, meet our niece Shreya she was here last week he said. I don't know how she would react as we had a bad partition and she kept on staring at me where I could see an ocean of love in her eyes hiding behind the silence. Meet my beta Ram said aunt Rekha grabbing my shoulder. We shook hands as strangers again where I felt the warmth on her palms. We had dinner talking things about my trip. I have shared about how I met Aarthi and our conversation throughout the flight where Uncle and Aunt remained silent, Shreya kept on staring at me without an expressionless face. I noticed a message from an unknown number after reaching home, it was from Shreya we had a long conversation about how my life turned out after we parted ways till how I landed up at her door. That night I kept on tossing on the bed to catch some sleep after meeting Shreya. Her eyes carrying the same emotions which I missed all these years felt like the answers which I have been searching over the years. I have decided to go out on a walk, the fresh 3 AM breeze, gushing sounds of the trees, the 9 degree temperature and my heart feeling normal after ages, the feeling of being myself back again had put on a smile on my face made the walk felt so special to me as I had spoken to myself for what my heart really craves for. I really feel like exploring the city where I was living from the past 4 years. I made myself a youngster had, Ice cream at a store, rode on a bicycle, stopping over the Pont De Calatrava bridge observing the cruise ships and boats sailing over. The next day I was at my office where aunt Rekha came with a wedding card and feeding me sweet. I opened the card excited to see a designer card baring the Indian style, My heart clutched to see the name of Shreya on it and I was disheartened again, then walked in Shreya dressed up in a red saree. Aunt Rekha said Invite Ram, Shreya with a huge smile on her face and She looked at me her eyes clearly stating that she was not really sure to marry that guy, words rolled out as she said you should definitely come Ram, I could clearly hear she stressing out my name.

Later that night I couldn't resist myself without texting her, I asked her whether she could come over to the park so that we could speak our hearts out. She said she will be there in 20 minutes. I quickly drove my Mercedes to the Parc De Cervantes. She came wrapped in a white coat, huge ear rings hanging down her ears and her cheeks turned red because of the freezing temperatures. You getting married, You didn't tell me yesterday in our chat? I shot my question straight away. I thought of telling that to you but aunt said she will take me to your office to invite her peers, so I didn't reveal she replied, in a kind of arrogant manner. Oh! It really surprised me, Umm Love marriage? I asked I stopped believing in love after you umm, she broke the words which were about to come and took a pause, I mean Its my parents choice and love has nothing to do with it she said. Okay I said Understanding the unspoken words that I have hurt her back in time. You like him, whats his name By the way I asked. Saurabh she said, He was a Pilot serving Indigo now she added. I said Cool and started to act normal where I started to understand that my heart wanting her. I couldn't bear anything like this says my brain and Look at her outspoken eyes she had got feelings for you, you are meant to be together saying my heart. I knew that apologizing her for what I have done in the past is the best thing to do before we leave as I don't want to end on a bad note. I'm really sorry for what I have done in the past Shreya I said, You don't have to be she said trying to control her emotions. Its late yaar Aunt would be worried Bye and its good to see you she said and started to walk back towards the exit of the park. I was stranded again in the pool of love unknowing whether she wants me or not and I couldn't ask that I was willing to hold her hand for the rest of my life. I started to build a strong gut feeling that I am not made for love and probably love is not my thing. I have to force myself to sleep by taking pills. What if I could win in this love story a chance popped up in my brain before my eyes got shut. Is this the revival of my life or am I taking a deep plunge?

TEN

UNSPOKEN LOVE

Barcelona,

I sat still in the wooden couch at Rekha aunts place where I could notice the very happy faces of the family around getting the preparations ready heading to India, I had a nervous feeling when Shreya was around and was very hesitant to talk to her, I spent most of the time with Rekha aunty helping her with the shopping for the wedding and with Shreya I had no conversations where our eyes kept on staring at each other as we fumble for words. I feel like everything my heart deserves is right in front of my eyes and was summoned and surrounded to defeat. I was eager to talk to her in private and texted her the day before she was leaving to India. She came to see me at the Parc De Cervantes at half past 10 in the night and she had carried a small paper bag with her, I didnt bother about that much Hey, Shreya whats happening with us, I didnt really like the feeling of wanting you, my heart is being crazy, it feels like I'm going to get into an another heart break. I cant figure it out what is the relation we had in between us. She had a sly smile on her face her hand slid into the bag which she brought along and she handed a book to me, It was the very personal book of mine where I used to have in my college days (remember the 2nd chapter?, If not you need to go back) It was my love notes? I was shocked to see it with her, she kept it with her all these years and she handed it now, what is it doing with you I asked and She replied, If you cannot be with me forever let your love be I thought and I kept it with me, now I believe I cannot keep it with me anymore. I got to go early morning flight she said and left where I felt like every step she takes is building the distance between us and It was pretty clear that It was love from her side, She loved me all her life and I never cared for her emotions back then, now I was desperate wanting her and time had different plans separating us. All I have was the love note handing down my heavy heart and my tears dropping on the leather strapped cover of the note. I sat all alone at the wooden bench in the park in the freezing cold temperature, Where my tear drops was the lone companion. I asked my driver to not to drop them to the airport as I would like to drop them personally. I have reached Rekha aunts place driving my Cadillac Escalade, I kept on staring at her in the mirror until we reach Josep Tarradellas Barcelona- El Prat Airport, She trying to avoid eye contact with me in all possible ways. Rekha aunt hugged me and whispered in my ear, If you didn't attend the wedding I wont talk to you anymore. I had smiled at her, uncle Deepak hugged me and waved me back. I looked at Shreya, It was probably the last time we could talk, She offered a handshake and was very reluctant to get hold of the handshake It clearly illustrated that she too was in love, the tear drop landed on my wrist melted my heart. Bye take care Ram please take care of yourself I'm so sorry she said before she left and I was left in silence as always. I woke up on the next day feeling exhausted. I went to office, made some designs for the upcoming project, attended the meetings with clients where my mind was completely absent, I have decided to speak with some of the old friends where the memories with them turned just into the contacts in my phone. Raghav was the first person I choose to call, He was amazed to see a call from me after ages, I spoke with him throughout my drive back home. My next ring was to Mahitha, living in the neighbouring country I never called or met her, I have spoken to her and her new born kid kept giggling and spoke broken words with me. I loved revisiting my old buddies and I pity myself not making an effort to reach them. Chasing dreams, running the rat race with life I lost lot of people in life who really meant a lot to me, where I turned people just into contacts in my phone. I figured one thing out that night, I was searching for love in one person I lost and ignoring all the people around. Then my heart wanted all the love which I lost back with time. I rushed to the airport and bought the next ticket to India. I decided to surprise my parents in the first place and really wanted to let Rekha aunt that Shreya and I were college mates and what is really going on in between us. I dozed off with anxiety kicking in and my hands wrapped around the love note which speaks the love between Shreya and me which went unspoken...

ELEVEN
WEDDING BELLS

New Delhi,

The sunny morning sunshine welcomed me with light winds brushing my hair as I stood right outside my home in Sector -B, Vasanthkunj. I slowly opened the long brown gate and made my way towards the main door. I was so excited while I was pressing the calling bell, My mom attended the door and was astonished to see me she hugged me tight, started crying aloud, She kept shouting at dad look who is here, Hamare Beta Ghar aagaya, My dad came running and hugged me tight, saying finally ghar yaad aaya. They missed me to the core so do I. I spoke with my parents all day, Had mom cooked food after ages. I told them about my trip to Canada and how I was living my life as of now. My parents were really proud of my success, After speaking about my career my dad asked me when are you getting married son, you are old enough to get married! I replied will let you know soon dad. It was the day of Shreya's wedding I asked my parents to come over aswell. I wrapped myself around in a navy blue tuxedo. Rekha aunt had welcomed my parents and she hugged me stating you look handsome today, but I will have to talk to you about Shreya you liar you guys even hid it from me. Her words took me by surprise, I walked through the extravagant wedding setup where Shreya along with so called Ronit who absolutely looked like a dumbass. I had met lot of my college juniors who were really really sweet even after years. My junior boys took me out for a smoke where I was speaking with them about the project models and my phone beeped, I noticed the call from Rekha aunt, She said Ram where are you come see me at the entrance, her voice seemed tensed. This call was certainly a hint that something had happened. I reached the entrance and couldnt find her I opened the first door and was about to grab the handle of the second one which leads to the convention area, The door got opened and the bride was walking out along with Shreya behind him, her eyes kept locked into mine as she was passing me and I was unaware of what was happening. Rekha aunt came to me and said that Shreya said she just stopped the wedding in between and told Ronit that she has to talk to him in private, they just went to talk and I don't understand what is going to happen. I went into the convention where everyone had question marked faces, Rekha aunt stood beside me where Shreya's parents were trying to convince Ronit's parents and family. After few minutes I headed towards where Shreya and Ronit were discussing. I took the steps and they were standing there Shreya saying something to Ronit, After noticing me Ronit came to me Shook hand with me and said You are the one for her brother, Ill manage my parents and family he said and turned towards Shreya said bye with a bright smile on his face. I was unknown about the situation and she stood still giving a romantic smile towards me she was dressed in light blue saree, the Indian bridal setup with lots of gold. She hugged me and said its time for our marriage my lovely husband, I too hugged back in excitement and said come lets get married. I hold her hand and we ran towards the Convention where Ronit had already convinced everyone there. I noticed some happy faces and some faces in disbelief, Rekha aunty and Deepak Uncle were so happy about us and my parents were busy inviting friends and family who were nearby. I Rekha aunt hugged me and said you even hid it form me but she told everything to me, umm I hate you for not telling me. I said I'm sorry aunt with my fingers holding my ears, That is how after all the chaos around the wedding hall I have tied the knot to my better half Shreya, We had invited everyone to our Reception Aarthi came along with Prudhvi and her daughter, my Grandparents, Raghav, Mahi, Dr. Karl from Canada and many other family and friends. Shreya and I were sitting on the fancy couple chair on the decorated stage in an expensive banquet hall. Shreya handed me the a small chit and asked me to read it later.

Epilogue

Its been 3 Years of my married life where Shreya and I were blessed with a baby girl, we were a happy family. Shreya was a perfect life partner and a great companion to live life with. We have cherished every little moment of our lives and the love we share was something which cannot be explained as everyone will have their chance to experience it, By the way did I tell you what was scribbled on that chit she gave in our reception? It scribbled " Go read your love note first, it wasn't the same as before" I have gone through every single page of it again where she had written every feeling of her about me, how she felt through every phase of our relation. I was surely in love as the last lines said, " No matter how far you go, what you do and how you are do remember that there is someone who loves you at the end of the day. You can never run away from love, dont search for love, embrace its presence around you. Love is a parasite which always feeds on a life, embrace it and experience the beauty of love", This is how I found my LOVE PARASITE.